HIGHLINERS

A Railroad Album

THE CHESAPEAKE AND OHIO'S TRAIN NO. 5-47, THE SPORTSMAN, WESTBOUND AT MAYSVILLE, KENTUCKY;
SUPER-PACIFIC NO. 484, SPEED APPROXIMATELY 70 M.P.H.

Lucius Beebe photograph

HIGHLINERS

A Railroad Album

by LUCIUS BEEBE

BONANZA BOOKS • NEW YORK

This edition published by Bonanza Books, a division of Crown Publishers, by arrangement with Meredith Publishing Company

h i j k l m n o

PRINTED IN THE UNITED STATES OF AMERICA

To

WILLIAM M. JEFFERS

of the UNION PACIFIC

FOREWORD

OVER a period of something more than a century and to hundreds of thousands, probably millions of people, the steam locomotive has been the most wonderful of all machines. It has dominated the American imagination as it has dominated the nation's economic destinies; as the ships of the world's oceans have laid hold upon the sensibilities of Englishmen since long before the time of Taliessin, the last Great Druid. As potent as the rifled firearm, as wealth-productive as the cotton-gin or the McCormick harvester and more beautiful than any other integrated mechanical devising of man's genius and necessity, the steam locomotive will forever haunt the human memory with its wonder.

The railroad train is an American institution evolved out of the urgent vastness of continental spaces and reaching its fullest flower almost with its first creation. It is one with the Mississippi River packet, the Bowie knife, the hook and ladder of the fire brigade, and peanuts at baseball games. Waving at trains is almost as purely American as carrying umbrellas is English. Railroads, locomotives, and the cars form a part of the earliest consciousness of youth just as they are one of the still fascinating commonplaces of maturity. And the steam locomotive is the archetypal symbol of all travel over the iron highroad.

FOREWORD

Only a brief six years before the publication of this book the first units of what were to be popularly if not precisely known as streamlined trains were delivered to the Union Pacific and the Chicago, Burlington and Quincy. The City of Salina, City of Portland, and Pioneer Zephyr were powered by internal combustion motors, designed along airflow lines and embodied altogether new structural principles in the fabrication of railroad equipment. Within a year fifteen passenger transport units of allied types were in process of construction, some of them steam-powered as were the Chicago and North Western's 400, the Milwaukee's Hiawathas, and the Baltimore and Ohio's Royal Blue, others, like the New Haven's Comet and the Alton's Abraham Lincoln, by Diesel-electric, while the Pennsylvania was content to place in service a series of electric engines of modified airflow design on the New York–Washington run. Various types of light-weight equipment both in motive power and rolling stock were purchased by every railroad which could afford the innovation; additional comforts and luxuries, in the form of air-conditioning, speeded-up schedules, and more privacy in sleeping accommodations were universally inaugurated, and the end is not yet in sight. Many of these in all categories of power and car construction were of arresting beauty; most of them at once demonstrated an ability, under suitable operating conditions, of increasing revenues, and one and all they laid hold upon a public imagination that, to a not inconsiderable extent, had allowed the legend of railroading to lapse into the sentimental discard.

It is not the purpose of this book to discuss the comparative merits, esthetic and technical, of modern and traditional schools of train design. It is sufficient that the evolution of a new variety of motive power with consequent mutations upon the equipment, style and spirit of railroading have revived a vast and unsuspected national affection for the tradition of rail transport and, by indirection, steam locomotion. It is not beyond the reach of a generous imagination

FOREWORD

that, when it has passed through its embryonic lack of definition, there may even be merit in the design of Diesel power. Not all change is necessarily retrogression. Old-time railroading has adequately been recorded in the still photographs so familiar to collectors, with the inclusion of their crews in mannered postures, bowler hats and oil cans prominently in view. With the coming of speed cameras and supersensitive films it has been possible to chronicle the most dramatic phases of contemporary railroading through the agency of action shots.

It has been the object of the author, therefore, to collect within these covers the best action photographs of modern trains which he was able to secure. In procuring them he has himself traveled not unimpressive distances, and he has called upon the resources of other photographers and never found them wanting either in generosity or enthusiasm for the work in hand. The perfect railroad action photograph—with its rural background, its clarity of definition of all moving parts, its indication of speed through smoke and steam exhaust, its full-length view of the entire train, and its absence of any object or matter to distract the attention from the locomotive and consist themselves—is not easy to come by. There are but a few hours each day when the flat light necessary for the clear depiction of valve motion and wheel arrangement is available, and long distances and inaccessible spots must frequently be achieved to meet these conditions. Often enough firemen, on seeing a cameraman by the right of way, abate as much as possible their smoke exhaust out of deference for the operations department's well-known prejudices in favor of a clear fire. Points of vantage for the cameraman are sometimes difficult of discovery, and the author has secured shots, upon occasion, more or less hazardously poised on fills and escarpments or depending from telegraph poles in a lineman's belt. Nor have railroad police ever entirely become reconciled to the amateur photographer.

If, in the preparation of this book, it is apparent that the author has evidenced

FOREWORD

an editorial prejudice in favor of several relatively unimportant railroads at the expense of the great trunk lines which span the continent, there are two reasons for the circumstance. The first is that in a previous volume of railroad photographs he attempted a more equitable geographic selection of picture material, and second, that his affections lie close to the less pretentious roads of the Middle and Southwest and their often far from up-to-the-minute equipment. The Wabash's Banner Blue and the Monon's Tippecanoe exercise for him a fascination not inherent in the grandeur of the Empire Builder or the Corn King. And although he has traveled often and spaciously on the Super Chief his heart has quickened and the breath caught in his throat for the approach across the Illinois meadows of the St. Louis Zipper as it has never done otherwise. For these reasons there are more photographs representing the Wabash, the Frisco and the Missouri Pacific than of the mighty New York Central and Southern Pacific combined. His better judgment may instruct him otherwise but he still believes that, esthetically speaking, a vintage Burlington muzzle-loader rolling through the Iowa cornlands with a cut of mixed freight stretching behind is more exciting than the Silver Meteor streaking southward under a winter sun at eighty miles an hour.

Railroad photography in its most satisfactory form is conditioned by a technique that is neither known nor understood by photographers honored and successful in other specialized fields of endeavor. There are conventions governing train photography as rigid as the unities of the French classic drama and as exacting as the uses of diplomatic protocol. Like any rules of established procedure, they have come into being not by authoritative fiat but by a process of evolution coincidental to the development of the subject they govern, and they are recognized by a limited but perceptive group of railroad students and historians.

PLATES

PLATES

PLATES

PLATES

HIGHLINERS

A Railroad Album

.1.

HAULING THE READING'S TONNAGE

Through the densely industrial regions of New Jersey and Pennsylvania with their vast manufactories and natural resources, the Reading handles an immense annual tonnage to and from the New York area. Most of its territory is comparatively level and as a result enormous loads are coupled behind its rumbling freight hogs. Near Roselle, New Jersey, with the overpass bridge of the Lehigh Valley in the background, this symmetrical Mikado is clattering down the outside iron with a mixed consist of 110 cars which will shortly engage in switching skirmishes in the Reading's vast classification yards outside Jersey City.

—Lucius Beebe photograph

. 2 .

VETERAN OF THE IOWA IRON

In France there are reported still to be in service locomotives built and placed in operation before the Franco-Prussian War, but in the United States it is a veritable Nestor of engines that has been in active main-line service for half a century. This Chicago, Burlington and Quincy veteran has been rolling up and down the iron of Iowa and Nebraska since the year 1888 and has covered a mileage which must be astronomical. It was photographed half a century after its maiden run on Extra 1261 Southbound at Fort Madison, Iowa, a city whose chief claim to fame in railroading annals is the location there of the Santa Fe's Shopton car and locomotive shops.

—William Barham–Ivan Oaks photograph

.3.

ROAD ENGINE AND HELPER

These heavy Pennsylvania freight hogs, a 2-10-2 running ahead of a giant 4-8-2, are handling one of the enormous drags of heavy consist which the Pennsy is accustomed to run as a single train rather than break it up into two smaller units. They are headed east near Logansport, Indiana, with 140-odd cars thundering behind at a good forty miles an hour.

—*Lucius Beebe photograph*

. 4 .

THE FABLED 400

The first 400, placed in service by the Chicago and North Western Railway between Chicago and the Twin Cities, Minnesota, in December, 1935, was a six-car train of conventional design with modern luxury fittings and hauled by reconditioned steam Pacifics on a schedule between Chicago and St. Paul carded for 400 miles in 400 minutes. It was the fastest long-haul train in the world. Four years later the North Western supplanted its standard equipment and steam power with eye-filling Diesel-powered units of airflow construction capable of a top speed of 117 miles an hour and combining every known comfort of daytime rail travel yet devised. There are formal dining-cars, low-priced lunch counters, tap rooms and card rooms, parlor cars, reclining seat coaches, and a smart observation lounge. There are stewardesses, morning-coated maîtres d'hôtel, and porters. The power of the 400 is a two-unit Diesel-electric locomotive, double-ended for switching and operating convenience, with a total of 4,000 horsepower, and the entire train is painted in a striking combination of bright yellow and deep green. This speed photograph shows the 400 (C. & N. W. Train No. 400) southbound near Eau Claire, Wisconsin.

—Chicago and North Western photograph

. 5 .

ALONG THE OHIO'S BANKS

In order to enlarge the firebox space of Consolidations and Decapods, Baldwin in 1897 designed for the Japanese Railways a locomotive with a 2-8-2 wheel arrangement in which the firebox was moved back from between the last pair of drivers and carried on a single pair of small trailing wheels. Because of their destination these engines were known as Mikados, an appellation which has ever since survived in abbreviated railroad jargon as "Mike." The Chesapeake and Ohio's enormous coal drags along the Ohio River are admirably suited to this type of power, and this photograph shows a C. & O. Mikado pulling out of Maysville, Kentucky, on the western haul after a brief water stop in the town. The head-end crew showed no reticence about being photographed as they highballed out of the yards.

—Lucius Beebe photograph

. 6 .

MIXED CONSIST

Powered by a heavy-duty Mikado with seventy cars of mixed consist nearing Brewster, Ohio, on the Cleveland run, this Wheeling and Lake Erie redball was snapped hitting forty miles an hour by Glen Grabill, Jr., constituting a dramatic photograph of tonnage action. The Mike is W. & L. E.'s No. 3005.

—*Railroad Photographs*

. 7 .

CATENARY AND PANTOGRAPH

The Class GG-1 electrics of the Pennsylvania constitute the most powerful electric passenger engines ever built. They are primarily designed to handle fast passenger traffic between New York, Philadelphia, Baltimore, Washington, and Harrisburg and are capable of sustained speed of 100 miles an hour with the heaviest sixteen and eighteen standard-car trains. The wheel arrangement is 4-6-0—0-6-4 and the total weight of such an engine is 477,000 pounds. Its maximum tractive effort is 72,800 pounds. The GG-1 shown here powers the Potomac on the Washington–New York run with a light cut of coaches and Pullmans near Princeton Junction, New Jersey. For general service the Pennsy maintains a fleet of electric locomotives classed as P-5a, a 4-6-4 type with a tractive force of 56,250 pounds, which are used interchangeably in freight and passenger hauls.

—Lucius Beebe photograph

. 8 .

SPIC AND SPAN CONSOLIDATION

This well-shopped Boston and Albany Consolidation (2-8-0) local freight hog is trailing a short cut of mixed consist along the Charles River at Faneuil, Massachusetts. The first consolidation was built by Baldwin for the Lehigh Valley in 1866 as an improvement over the wheel arrangements and steaming capacities of the eight-wheelers and Moguls theretofore used for freight service. Nowadays Consolidations are largely used for switching and in branch-line service, their boiler capacity, for lack of a trailer truck to support the firebox, being insufficient for long hauls of heavy trains.

—Lucius Beebe photograph

.9.

THE FRISCO'S SUNNYLAND

The St. Louis-San Francisco Railway's No. 107, the Sunnyland, with drawing-room and sleeping-cars from Denver to Atlanta via Denver and Rio Grande Western, Missouri Pacific, Frisco, and Birmingham and Southern Railway, heads out of St. Louis behind Frisco light Pacific No. 1038 with a tall stack and high domes to indicate its venerable vintage.

—William Barham–Ivan Oaks photograph

. 10 .

"GET A HORSE!"

Railroad men and amateurs who believe in conventional steam power and have little use for the devisings of modernity in the form of Diesel and electric engines, are never so enchanted as when a Diesel unit fails to function and its train has to be taken over by the iron horse of old. In justice to the builders of internal-combustion motors, it should be remarked that this is a less frequent occurrence than it was when Diesel power was in its railroading infancy only a few years ago, but here is the proud General Pershing Zephyr of the Alton-Burlington run between Denver and St. Louis shamefully being helped on its way by an aging Burlington Pacific near Sheffield, Missouri. In a prouder moment the General Pershing Zephyr will be found rolling on its gleaming way on a subsequent page.

—Lucius Beebe photograph

. 11 .

Zephyrus, the West Wind, has been the nominal archetype of the Chicago, Burlington and Quincy's famed series of Zephyrs, Diesel-powered, light-weight, speedy passenger hauls ranging in coverage from the Northwest states to deepest Texas. The Denver Zephyr, in competition to the Union Pacific's City of Denver on the Chicago run, is the Q's de luxe venture; the Sam Houston Zephyr, ranging between Fort Worth–Dallas and Houston, its southernmost daily pacemaker. This is the General Pershing unit which includes in its consist standard Pullmans as well as the lightweight equipment characteristic of its class. On the St. Louis, Kansas City and Lincoln run, the General Pershing Zephyr makes a round trip daily of 978 miles at an average overall speed of 55.8 miles an hour. Here it is shown rolling southward of a hot July noon near St. Louis.

—*Lucius Beebe photograph*

. 12 .

"ON THE ADVERTISED"

Esteemed by many railroad amateurs and technicians as the handsomest in design of all Diesel-powered fleets, the Baltimore and Ohio's Columbian, Capitol Limited, and Royal Blue are painted the deep blue and silver that is the B. & O.'s hallmark and flash across the countryside to the sonorous thunder of their internal-combustion power units. The Royal Blue, shown on the opposite page, is the glory of the B. & O.'s New York–Washington service. It includes in its consist a café-lounge-observation car, drawing-room parlor cars, a formal diner and a tavern-counter-buffet, and individual reclining chair coaches with the added feature of a ladies' lounge and combine car. Here the Royal Blue is picking up speed as she rolls gleamingly through Plainfield over the tracks of the Central Railroad of New Jersey before crossing to the B. & O.'s own iron at Bound Brook, New Jersey.

—Lucius Beebe photograph

. 13 .

WAITING FOR THE GREEN BOARD

Behind these two engine drivers, one of a conventional New York, New Haven and Hartford Pacific, the other at the controls of a Diesel switcher in Boston's South Station, looms the whole tradition of American railroading. As they pause, on adjacent tracks, waiting to roll into the main, there stand back of them many generations of bearded hoggers and high-wheel artists who drove their power across the width of a continent and created with their exploits at throttle and Johnson bar one of the most romantic of all sagas. They wheeled their hotshots over the new-laid iron through Laramie and North Platte and, with four Mogul helpers, they thundered through the passes of Glorieta and Raton when the deep Southwest was young. They were then, as they are now, the archetypal railroad men, the central figures of the exhaust-cadenced epic of the high iron.

—H. W. Pontin photograph

. 14 .

COURIER OF THE NORTH WOODS

The supposedly archaic high-wheeled Atlantic-type (4-4-2) locomotive came into its own again for high-speed passenger runs a few years ago when the Chicago, Milwaukee, St. Paul and Pacific created the first Hiawathas on the Chicago–Minneapolis haul as direct competition to the North Western's 400. The daily mileage per train is 422 accomplished (on the Chicago–St. Paul run) at an average of 63.1 miles an hour. Starting as a six-car train, the afternoon Hiawatha is now a standard nine-car flyer, often hauling as many as fourteen cars. Original equipment and locomotives have been replaced, and the train revenue per mile averages the astonishingly high figure of $3.80. All the conveniences of a de luxe daytime haul, including a unique "beaver tail" observation car, are found aboard the Hiawatha, which is here shown hitting seventy-five as it streaks through Forest Preserve, Illinois, on a cold winter day.

—R. H. Kennedy, Jr., photograph

. 15 .

ILLINOIS CENTRAL DRAG

The Illinois Central's motive power is seldom a joy to railroad men conscious of the esthetic possibilities of locomotive design, but its fast freight service from Chicago south and west, through the agency of such passenger-schedule redballs as PD-1 and MS-1, served to step up the freight cardings of every competing road in the Middle West. Here is a less celebrated drag, powered by one of the I. C.'s powerful mountain-type engines, breasting a slight grade with seventy cars of mixed merchandise near Mattoon, Illinois, under a July noontide sun.

—Lucius Beebe photograph

. 16 .

MALLET MIGHT AND MOTION

The Southern Pacific's cab-first Mallets are as characteristic of the road as its car herald (almost universal in California) its snowsheds in the High Sierras, or its nearly complete dominance of the passenger haul trade into San Francisco proper, where its only rivals are the Santa Fe and Western Pacific across the bay at Oakland. Improved visibility, especially on sharp curves, and a reduction of exhaust nuisance to engine crews in tunnels and snowsheds are the basis of cab-first design, and these 4-8-8-2 Mallets are familiar wherever the Espee iron reaches in California and Nevada. It will readily be seen how placing the smokestack behind the cab instead of ahead of it must contribute to the comfort of engine crews in the long, close Sierra tunnels, and in this photograph the fireman is leaning out of the window backward to view his smoke. Train 2-26 is the second section of the Owl on the San Francisco–Los Angeles run, and it is shown a few miles below Glendale on a fine summer's morning.

—G. M. Best photograph

. 17 .

THE ALTON'S NO. 18, ANN RUTLEDGE

Named for Abraham Lincoln's first love and the fastest of all steam passenger trains on the Chicago–St. Louis run, the Ann Rutledge covers the 282 miles between America's greatest railroad centers in four hours and fifty-five minutes or at an average of a little better than fifty-seven miles an hour. Headed by Pacific No. 5293 with eight streamlined coaches and chair cars in tow, it is shown gathering speed just north of the east approach tower to the Merchant's Bridge at Granite City, Illinois. The Rutledge's complementary train on the Chicago–St. Louis run is the Abraham Lincoln, a Diesel-powered unit, but the train's equipment first saw service on the Baltimore and Ohio's New York–Washington run in 1934.

—Lucius Beebe photograph

. 18 .

ALONG THE LOUISVILLE & NASHVILLE

The Louisville and Nashville's Dixie Limited, Train 92, westbound, with sleeping-cars from Jacksonville to Chicago and from Atlanta to St. Louis and a full consist of coaches, diners, observation and lounge cars, is powered by Pacific No. 240 on the L. & N. roster, as it sweeps around a woodland curve coming into East St. Louis. The L. & N.'s iron reaches from Cincinnati to New Orleans with Memphis, Atlanta, and St. Louis as branch-line terminals. Other crack varnish trains on its operating schedules are the Crescent, Flamingo, Southland and Piedmont Limited.

—William Barham–Ivan Oaks photograph

.19.

THE BEAUTY OF THE CHIEF

Although the Atchison, Topeka and Santa Fe's Diesel-powered Super Chief may actually top it in ingenious luxuries and beauty of appointments, the road's Chief still constitutes in the minds of thousands of transcontinental travelers a standard of railroad opulence all its own. It makes the Los Angeles–Chicago run over the mountain passes of the Cajon, Glorieta, and Raton, the uplands of Colorado, and the plains of Kansas in 59½ hours, complete with every devising of de luxe modernity including the celebrated food and service of Harvey restaurant cars. This is The Chief running into San Bernardino, California, behind one of the Santa Fe's 3765 Series Northern (4-8-4) locomotives which will haul it without change of motive-power as far as La Junta, Colorado.

—Lucius Beebe photograph

. 20 .

INTO THE CUMBRES

This straight-stacked Denver and Rio Grande Western 2-8-2, No. 485 narrow-gage locomotive is heading an extra of heavy merchandise as it heads into the Cumbres Pass near Los Piños, Colorado. Behind, with its smoke rolling over the timbered uplands, is No. 484. The photograph, so reminiscent of railroading in the silver lode frontiers of yesterday, was, in fact, taken in the summer of 1939 and is a tribute to the vitality of the narrow-gage tradition in the West.

—*R. H. Kindig photograph*

. 21 .

A RARE 4-4-4

This Baltimore and Ohio No. 1 is a rare design in modern steam power with a 4-4-4 wheel arrangement. It was built in 1936 and assigned to passenger service on the Cleveland-Wheeling run after experimental hauls on other divisions. It was photographed by Glenn Grabill, Jr., getting under way in the yards outside Warwick, Ohio, bound for Cleveland.

—Railroad Photographs

. 22 .

ALONG THE KANSAS CITY SOUTHERN

The K. C. Southern's Train No. 1 is shown here powered by an unusually grace-ful and carefully tended Pacific whose silver-painted cylinder heads and green-black, mirror-like boiler shell are evidences of recent shopping and diligent servicing by roundhouse crews. Her airflow lounge, dining- and chair-cars are painted a deep, glossy green and boast hostess service, attractive menus, and much of the luxury of more celebrated day-passenger hauls. On the run to Shreveport, Louisiana, No. 1 is rolling briskly southward on the tracks of the Kansas City Terminal near Sheffield, Missouri.

—Lucius Beebe photograph

.23.

IN NORTHERN CALIFORNIA

The Super-Mountain-type locomotive here shown wheeling eastward near Sacramento through the farmlands of northern California with the Western Pacific's Scenic Limited in tow was originally built for the Florida East Coast Railroad (Flagler System). Equipped with a new stack, smoke deflector and other devices and numbered 177 on the W. P.'s roster it powers the road's crack varnish on the run over the Feather River Route to meet the iron of the Denver and Rio Grande Western at Salt Lake. Completed in 1911, the W. P. was the last great piece of transcontinental railroad building in the United States and runs in competition to the Southern Pacific in Utah, Nevada, and California as far as Oakland Pier. Edward N. Bewley caught the Scenic against a typical background for Railroad Photographs.

—*Railroad Photographs*

. 24 .

SUPER CHIEF SYMBOL

Generally considered the last word in super-luxury trains along with such transcontinental highliners as the City of Los Angeles and Forty-niner, the Atchison, Topeka and Santa Fe's Super Chief is a name world-famous as a synonym with de luxe and speedy travel. An extra-fare, all-Pullman limited on the Chicago–Los Angeles run, it covers two-thirds of the North American continent in thirty-nine and a half hours with a revenue per train mile of $2.22. It is a favorite with stage and film celebrities and so great is its prestige that its sailing list during the winter months is full for weeks in advance. It abounds in lounges, club cars, and other non-revenue units, and its decorative scheme is the last word in smart, modernistic simplicity with a Navajo motif. This elevation of the Super Chief's prow was made as the train stopped briefly at La Junta, Colorado, for servicing and inspection.

—Lucius Beebe photograph

. 25 .

ON SCHEDULE: C. & E. I. NO. 93

Highballing out of Chicago in mid-afternoon on the Florida run with connections over the iron of the Louisville and Nashville, N. C. & St. L., Atlantic Coast Line and Florida East Coast, the Dixie Limited on the Chicago and Eastern Illinois finds the board is green as it passes through Lincoln Fields, Illinois, on the advertised behind Pacific No. 1018.

—R. H. Kennedy, Jr., photograph

.26.

UP FROM THE OZARKS

rolls the Frisco's Meteor, burnished and gleaming in the morning sunlight at Glendale, a few minutes' run from the St. Louis yards. Like the Texas Special, Bluebonnet, Sunnyland, Memphian and other St. Louis–San Francisco trains, both power and equipment on the Meteor are magnificently immaculate as to paint, varnish, and metal. The Frisco's Mountain-type locomotives are among the handsomest extant, and the history of the road is closely entwined with the Missouri legend and the saga of the great Southwest. Much of its own power is built at the Springfield shops, and its iron spreads a network over Missouri and Oklahoma and reaches as far south as Fort Worth in Texas and Pensacola in Florida.

—Lucius Beebe photograph

.27.

IN THE COLORADO ROCKIES

This impressive Mallet, No. 3607 on the roster of the Denver and Rio Grande Western, was caught near Pando, Colorado, by R. H. Kindig, climbing the 3 per cent grade of Tennessee Pass with fifty-odd cars of hot merchandise behind. The train was preparing to head in at Pando (note the brakeman coming out of the cab window to ride front end of the engine to the switch) to let the eastbound Scenic run around No. 36. At the rear end of the train No. 3614 was helping roll the hotshot over the top.

—*R. H. Kindig photograph*

. 28 .

GOLDEN AND GLEAMING: THE BLUE BONNET

Synonymous with meticulous grooming is the maintenance of rolling stock and motive-power of the St. Louis–San Francisco Railway. Even in a region where trains still gleam with gold and red and varnish in the old manner, the Frisco's freight and passenger locomotives alike are celebrated for their valve motion and rods, the blue-gray sheen of their boiler housings, the golden bells and the red trim of their markers. Here is the slickest of the Frisco's flyers, the Blue Bonnet, rolling west at Osage Hills, Missouri. It is powered by a streamlined Pacific, No. 1026, and a Mountain-type road engine, No. 1509. In the Ozarks the Frisco's trains possess a hold on the popular imagination closely akin to that which the Century, the Ghost Train on the New Haven, and the Overland held for the entire country only yesterday.

—William Barham–Ivan Oaks photograph

. 29 .

PRIDE OF THE SEABOARD

Powered by the mightiest Diesel units in operation in the East and running between New York and Miami in twenty-six and a quarter hours, the Seaboard Railway's Orange Blossom Special is the classic passenger train to Florida. All Pullman, completely air-conditioned and air-cooled, equipped with tight-locking couplers, rubber draft gear, and devices for eliminating all slack between cars, the Orange Blossom provides de luxe accommodations complete with luxury lounges, observation cars, and diners. The Diesel-power shown hauling the Orange Blossom consists of three units of 2,000 horsepower each. It is 210 feet long and weighs 900,000 pounds and requires but two fuel stops on the run between Washington and South Florida. This is Train No. 8 on the Seaboard, northbound, near West Palm Beach.

—Lucius Beebe photograph

. 30 .

NOT ESTHETICS BUT UTILITY

Neither the old-time glory of steam power nor the sleek modernity of Diesel design are characteristic of this Union Pacific gas-electric motor mail train, M-66. It serves its useful purpose, however, in operation on the Manhattan Division of the Kansas Branch, making all mail stops and picking up none on the fly as is indicated by the absence of a steel arm for grabbing sacks from trackside stands. The photograph was taken when M-66 was on the run between Lincoln, Nebraska, and Council Bluffs as it passed through the Omaha yards.

—Lucius Beebe photograph

. 31 .

Rolling over the neatly manicured roadbed of the Canadian National at Dixie Station, Province of Quebec, and flying the white flags of an extra, this heavy duty 4-8-4, with continental-type smoke deflectors and its bell mounted on the left of the boiler shell, is allowing no slack in the draft gear of seventy carloads of mixed consist. Despite a speed of forty miles an hour its stack shows no exhaust, a circumstance that is gratifying to railroad executives but no cause for satisfaction to railroad photographers.

—Railroad Photographs

. 32 .

THE FLORIDA SPECIAL

During the winter season at Palm Beach, Boca Raton, and Miami, when vacationists are filling every Florida resort hotel and club, the Atlantic Coast Line's Florida Special sometimes rolls south with eighteen Pullmans over the rails of the Pennsylvania, the Richmond, Fredericksburg and Potomac, and the Florida East Coast Line (the Flagler system). It makes the run from New York to Miami between 1:15 P.M. daily and 3:30 the following afternoon, and to maintain this schedule, often in several heavy sections, it runs double shotted as shown in this action photograph, over the Flagler iron, between Fort Lauderdale and Hollywood, Florida.

—*Lucius Beebe photograph*

. 33 .

MAILS ON THE MOPAC

These giant Mountain-type (4-8-2) locomotives are standard power on the southern and western lines of the Missouri Pacific running out of St. Louis. Shortly after sunrise each morning, No. 5 sets out for Kansas City, Omaha, and Lincoln with a string of mail and express cars and three or four through Pullmans and coaches. Here her engine driver is coasting down a slight grade a few miles west of Webster Groves, Missouri.

—Lucius Beebe photograph

. 34 .

NEARING ST. LOUIS TERMINAL

Famed in railroad legend is the Wabash, training school for many generations of railroad operatives and executives. It is the oldest line in continual service in the Middle West, and the verb "to Wabash," in railroad language, is synonymous with fast and fancy running. Shown at speed at Granite City, Illinois, is the road's crack daytime passenger flier, the Banner Blue on the Chicago–St. Louis run. The Pacific locomotives of this series are all in excess of thirty years old, but so carefully have they been serviced that they are good for many more years of fast and economical running.

—Lucius Beebe photograph

. 35 .

ROCK ISLAND IDYL

This Chicago, Rock Island and Pacific 2-8-2 with its exhaust standing straight up into the summer sky presents a pleasant railroad pastoral as it hauls No. 93 over the single iron near Farmington, Iowa. As incidentals to this idyllic scene cattle graze in the clovered meadows and the swing brakeman takes his ease aloft on a box car in the middle of the train.

—William Barham–Ivan Oaks photograph

. 36 .

THE FLYING CROW

From Kansas City Terminal through Missouri, Oklahoma, Arkansas, and Louisiana to Port Arthur, Texas, a distance of 788 miles, runs the iron of the Kansas City Southern Lines. Its revenue derives from the rich agricultural products of the deep South and from the merchandise shipped on the Gulf of Mexico. Its principal daily varnish is the Flying Crow, shown here thundering north near Grandview, Missouri, under a heavy cloud of smoke exhaust, her cylinder heads and smokebox door painted a gleaming silver.

—Lucius Beebe photograph

. 37 .

MISSOURI PACIFIC SUPERPOWER

This dramatic action shot shows the Missouri Pacific's 2-10-2, No. 1702, as lead engine and No. 1913, a heavy 2-8-4 or Berkshire type, as road engine on No. 75, the Red Ball, at Webster Groves, Missouri. It constitutes a handsome action photograph of midwestern railroading with modern superpower units in full swing.

—William Barham–Ivan Oaks photograph

.38.

HOTSHOT OUT OF TEXAS

William Barham, a St. Louis motorcycle police officer, and his associate, Ivan Oaks, make a specialty of action photography along the lines running out of their native city: Mopac, Frisco, Wabash, Chicago and Eastern Illinois, Alton, Louisville and Nashville and such, and have produced some of the most distinguished railroad pictures of the generation. Here is one of their action shots of the St. Louis–San Francisco's No. 4309, a newly built Mountain-type freight hog ahead of Train No. 38, the Texas Live Stock, eastbound at Kirkwood, Missouri.

—William Barham–Ivan Oaks photograph

. 39 .

SERVICE FOR SIDE RODS

The traditional picture of the locomotive engineer, flaring torch in one hand and long snouted oil can in the other, lubricating the running parts of his engine as it pauses in the night, has by no means disappeared from the railroading scene, but on modern engines most crossheads in their guide bars are lubricated by elaborate automatic oiling systems and on giant road engines such as this the bearings are serviced with steam-actuated grease guns which are a far cry from the mutton tallow smear which originally gave the fireman the name of "tallowpot." At service stops on transcontinental hauls these grease guns are attached to a steam line on the locomotive and grease cartridges are fed into them much as ammunition is fed into an automatic rifle. The photograph shows two members of a Union Pacific service crew, one handling the gun itself while the other stands by with a supply of cartridges, lubricating the side rod bearings on an intermediate driving wheel of a 4-8-2 attached to the Overland Limited at Laramie.

—Lucius Beebe photograph

. 40 .

ON THE WINGS OF THE MORNING

Gleaming with brown, yellow, and gold and flying the symbols of the Chicago and North Western, Union Pacific, and Southern Pacific Railroads, the City of San Francisco, the last word in super de luxe varnish fliers, climbs, behind snarling Diesels, into the approaches of the Wasatch. Behind is Ogden, Utah; ahead the grades, curves, fills, and tunnels of one of the most difficult divisions of the Overland Route. Complete with luxury lounges, private suites, glittering restaurants, and every travel luxury known to modern design, the City of San Francisco, like its sister train, the City of Los Angeles, is a miracle of mechanical resource and decorative ingenuity. Its fourteen passenger cars are staffed with porters and valets, barbers, maids, maîtres d'hôtel, wine stewards, waiters, and secretaries, and no refinement of pleasure or convenience is omitted in its economy. The only indication of the eighty miles an hour it is making here is the dust cloud rising under its trucks.

—Lucius Beebe photograph

. 41 .

A HOGGER WORKS UP SPEED

In the twenty-five miles between San Bernardino, California, and Summit, where the helper engines are usually cut out, the Puerto del Cajon rises 2,750 feet. Actually the grade is sharper than is indicated by these figures, since for five or six miles east of San Bernardino yards the tracks of the Atchison, Topeka and Santa Fe lie straight across gently rising meadows where it is possible to work up momentum for the pull into the Cajon itself. Over these rolling uplands it is customary for the trains of the Santa Fe and the Union Pacific, which uses the Santa Fe iron from Barstow to San Bernardino, to streak with the throttle notched back as far as the driver cares to hold it. This dramatic action shot by G. M. Best shows U. P. X5518 with white flags flying hitting the hills behind a Super 2-10-2, while in the middle of the train and at its end there are helpers.

—Railroad Photographs

.42.

A STUDY IN SUPERLATIVES

Any description of the Southern Pacific Lines' twin Daylight streamliners entails a number of superlatives. They have been designated and rank in the minds of many people as "the most beautiful trains in the world." They are the most luxurious means of long-distance travel anywhere in the West, and they are the among the most profitable passenger trains of all time, grossing nearly five dollars per train mile and having carried more than 100,000 fares in their first 135 days of operation. And, although the Espee can scarcely be credited with the circumstance, they traverse on the San Francisco–Los Angeles run one of the most varied and scenic of railroad hauls. Because the Daylights often ran in as many as four sections, the Southern Pacific was forced to order two additional complete train units to maintain the standard of their equipment and schedule. The specially designed locomotives, built by Lima, are of the GS-3 classification with a 4-8-4 wheel arrangement, and the trains cost a cool million dollars a unit. Their luxury of tavern and restaurant cars, coffee-shops, lounges, cafés, and other non-revenue equipment equal those of such de luxe flyers as the Congressional, Yankee Clipper, 400, and celebrated daylight hauls. Here is the northbound first section topping seventy in the Salinas Valley.

—Lucius Beebe photograph

.43.

ROLLING TOWARD CINCINNATI

Ahead of a mixed consist of company coal, high cars and other heavy freight rolling stock, this Texas type (2-10-4) hog of the Chesapeake and Ohio's 3000 class presents a striking representation of heavy duty motive power in action.

—Railroad Photographs

. 44 .

THE BELT RAILROAD'S ONE SPOT

This serviceable looking Santa Fe (2-10-2) locomotive with a mighty drag of mixed freight and empties behind it and equipped with a hopper-type tender and footboards for yard, shifting, and transfer duty is the Belt Railroad of Chicago's No. 1. Photographed one winter morning ascending the hump at Clearing, Illinois, by R. H. Kennedy, Jr., of Chicago, it presents a dramatic picture of heavy-duty freight transfer power in action. The Belt Railroad serves as a clearing and transfer agency for freight on the many roads which radiate from Chicago toward every point of the geographic and industrial compass.

—R. H. Kennedy, Jr., photograph

. 45 .

SUBSTITUTE POWER

When the streamlined, speedy Pacific, precise counterpart save for its sheathing, of the engine shown here, which customarily hauls the Reading's Crusader, is in the shops the run is taken over by Pacific No. 178 which is usually assigned to the run of the Seven O'Klocker. Trailing the Crusader's Budd-built, sightly coaches, No. 178, with its characteristic flanged stack and concealed pumps and lubricators, is topping seventy as it heads down the straightaway that stretches westward out of Elizabeth, New Jersey.

—Lucius Beebe photograph

.46.

CRUSADER AT CRUISING SPEED

From the Jersey City Terminal to Philadelphia aboard the Reading Lines' stainless steel streamlined flyer, the Crusader, consumes but an hour and thirty-eight minutes, and passengers enjoy the luxury of the most modern appointments, individual reclining seat coaches, observation lounge, restaurant car with cocktail lounge, and every convenience of speedy daylight travel at the regular coach fare. One of the most esthetically satisfactory of trains of airflow design, the Crusader maintains an overall scheduled speed of a mile a minute and is here shown hitting it up on the main line one winter morning just outside the Jersey City Terminal yards.

—Lucius Beebe photograph

. 47 .

ONCE ALONG THE ESPEE

Train No. 12, the Apache, eastbound, is no longer to be found upon the Southern Pacific's operating schedules. Its identity and services have been merged in other passenger hauls over the Sunset Route. Until her graveyard run, however, a few years ago, the Apache was a good example of mixed mail, express, coach, and Pullman train which wheeled its not too hasty way across the deserts of Arizona and New Mexico to Tucumcari where it joined the Rock Island for the run to Chicago. Here it is shown with a string of venerable equipment behind a well-groomed 4-8-2 near Palm Springs, California.

—Lucius Beebe photograph

. 48 .

VIGNETTE OF YESTERDAY

Although in actual fact only taken in 1938, this is a picture out of the old heroic past of western railroading when the narrow-gage roads were an integral part of the legend of the high iron. It shows a Colorado and Southern freight powered by two 2-8-0 narrow-gage engines, Nos. 70 and 73, on the high bridge of the Georgetown Loop, en route from Denver to Silver Plume. To-day the line has been abandoned and the bridge removed, but the canyon it crossed will forever be peopled with the memories of the little trains that shared in its romance.

—R. H. Kindig *photograph*

. 49 .

DAY VARNISH SOUTH

With her exhaust pounding skyward, the Chicago, Indianapolis and Louisville Railroad's Tippecanoe highballs out of the Englewood Station, Chicago, on the Monon's midday run to Indianapolis, Indiana, 183 miles to the south.

—Lucius Beebe photograph

. 50 .

GREEN AND SILVER OF THE MAPLELEAF

The Grand Trunk Railway's No. 8, the Mapleleaf, on the Chicago-Toronto-Montreal run, gleams brilliant with contrasting shades of green and silver as it rolls eastward near South Bend, Indiana. A pool train between Toronto and Montreal, the Mapleleaf's power is a 4-8-4, built along airflow lines with a novel smoke deflector and partly sheathed valve motion. The Grand Trunk operates 1,224 miles of road in the United States while its parent road, the Canadian National, embraces 21,800 miles of iron highway in the Dominion of Canada. Other famed passenger runs on the Grand Trunk are those of the Continental Limited, the Maritime Express, the Inter-City Limited and the Gull. Six of these streamlined, Lima-built 4-8-4s are in operation between Chicago and Port Huron.

—Lucius Beebe photograph

. 51 .

FACING THE SUNSET

Awash with looped and fringed drawing room curtains, mahogany woodwork, and the solid comfort of yesterday's Pullmans, the Illinois Central's Daylight on the Chicago–St. Louis run rolls up the approach to the Merchant's Bridge, just east of the Granite City interlocking at twilight. Fast and luxurious in the old manner, the Daylight competes on this run with the Chicago and Eastern Illinois's St. Louis Zipper, the Wabash's Banner Blue and the Alton Limited, each of which are pictured elsewhere in this book. From the condition of the roadbed as indicated on the opposite page it would seem that the Terminal Railroad of St. Louis, whose iron is shown, might well invest in a weed-burner.

—Lucius Beebe photograph

. 52 .

EAST FROM OMAHA

rolls the Union Pacific–Chicago and North Western's many cars of the Pacific Limited with a full quota of fifteen baggages, coaches, and Pullmans. The power is one of the Chicago and North Western's sightly, streamlined, super steam units, Hudson-type No. 4002, one of the most impressive designs of steam locomotive on any roster. The photograph, showing the Limited rolling out of the Omaha yards on the Chicago run, was taken by R. H. Kindig from an adjacent signal tower.

—Courtesy of Railroad Magazine

. 53 .

MAILS FOR DENVER

No. 9 is the westbound section of the Burlington's overnight mail between Omaha and Denver. Powered by a sleek Burlington 4-8-2 and a minute or two off schedule, it is shown hitting close to eighty miles an hour between Eno and Denver with three mail-and-baggage coaches and a brace of Pullmans in leash. A few hours previous, the Burlington's crack luxury streamliner, the Denver Zephyr, has rolled into the Colorado uplands over the same division with its profitable quota of passengers and through mail from Chicago and the East.

—Lucius Beebe photograph

. 54 .

LACKAWANNA LOCAL

Photographed by famed railfan Thomas T. Taber of Madison, New Jersey, this sleek rebuilt Pacific of the Delaware, Lackawanna and Western Railroad has been taken off the main line and placed in suburban service where it is shown hauling a local near Montclair, New Jersey. The principal through trains on the Lackawanna are the Lackawanna Limited, the Westerner, and the Chicago Limited which connect at Buffalo with the Nickel Plate for Chicago.

—Courtesy of Railroad Magazine

. 55 .

THE GLORY OF THE ROCK ISLAND

The Golden State Limited, crack transcontinental luxury highliner of the Chicago, Rock Island and Pacific Railway, rolls into Englewood station at Chicago after a run of 2,340 miles over the iron of the Rock Island and Southern Pacific roads. Over the Golden State Route the Rock Island's main line runs across corners of Iowa and Missouri to meet the Espee at Tucumcari, New Mexico. Its passenger service offers a more leisurely run than that of the Santa Fe or Union Pacific into Los Angeles, but its de luxe trains, such as the Golden State, are staffed with a full complement of maids and valets, barkeeps, stewards, and barbers, and its equipment includes standard Pullmans, modern streamlined chair cars, diners, lounges, cafés, and observation cars. Its run through the deep South-west is one of the most spectacular tours of the Indian country of Arizona and New Mexico.

—Lucius Beebe photograph

. 56 .

COLORADO AND SOUTHERN

Running double-headed, this Colorado and Southern (Burlington Lines) tourist special is heading for Denver over the Colorado countryside after an overnight run from Cody, Wyoming, and the Yellowstone Park. Its power comprises two Pacifics of conventional Burlington design and familiar everywhere along the Burlington Route, including the Colorado and Southern and Fort Worth and Denver City Railway Companies.

—Lucius Beebe photograph

. 57 .

THE GEORGIA RAILROAD SHOWS ITS SPEED

Streaking along under a plume of black exhaust smoke near Decatur, Georgia, the Georgia Railroad's Atlanta–Augusta local is caught hitting fifty by Richard E. Prince, Jr., as well-tended Pacific No. 254 does its stuff on the power end of the seven-car train.

—Courtesy of Railroad Magazine

. 58 .

B. & O. EXPERIMENT

Before the Baltimore and Ohio adopted the Diesel unit which now powers the Royal Blue on the New York–Washington run, this streamlined train was hauled by a steam unit designed along airfoil lines and shown here streaking toward the Washington yards with the electrified tracks of the Pennsylvania just out of the photograph on the right.

—*W. R. Osborne photograph*

. 59 .

ON THE PASSING TRACK

The Illinois Central's celebrated fast merchandise, P. D. 1, powered by Mikado No. 1464 is on the passing track at fifteen miles an hour at Jackson, Mississippi, while No. 3 rolls by at thirty on the south main. The head shack of P. D. 1 rides the footboard of the pilot to throw the switch into the main when No. 3 has gone its way. As far as appearance is concerned, the I. C.'s freight power would seem more carefully tended than its passenger hogs.

—C. William Witbeck photograph

. 60 .

THE KATY'S NO. 6

The only Missouri-Kansas-Texas passenger train that runs out of St. Louis is the Katy Flyer. Because of the heavy grades on this division the more conventional passenger power of a Pacific or Mountain-type is dispensed with in favor of a Mikado freight locomotive which is shown at Prospect Hill, Missouri. Three passenger cars, two coaches, and a Pullman trail behind the four mail cars on this run.

—William Barham–Ivan Oaks photograph

. 61 .

QUEEN OF THE VALLEY

From Bound Brook, New Jersey, eastward through Plainfield, Cranford, and Elizabeth, the New York–bound trains of the Baltimore and Ohio and the Reading run over the iron of the Central Railroad of New Jersey, making it one of the busiest rights of way in the entire country where towermen are forever alert to handle the dense traffic of three roads with their freights, mainliners, and commuting trains. Its stretches are populous with many types of power, the ancient camelbacks of the C. of N. J., the gleaming Diesel flyers of the B. & O., the thunderous Mikados and semi-streamlined Pacifics of the Reading. Here is the C. of N. J.'s Queen of the Valley, fast carded varnish on the Harrisburg–Newark run, trailing coaches, Pullmans, and a club-diner at a good seventy-five near Cranford. Its power is a recently shopped heavy Pacific, No. 820.

—Lucius Beebe photograph

. 62 .

"HE CLIMBED TO THE CAB WITH HIS ORDERS
IN HIS HAND"

As in the ballad of Casey Jones, this modern ballast scorcher has compared his train orders and railroad Hamilton with the conductor and is prepared to wheel the Chicago and Eastern Illinois' crack Dixieland out of Danville, Illinois, as soon as his fireman confirms the clear board by shouting "Highball." His power is a beautifully maintained Pacific with polished rod assembly, nickel steel cylinder heads and immaculate boiler lagging. Above the drop coupler its name shows that No. 1023 is dedicated to serving the Dixieland alone during the winter months, and none but an irreverent engine foreman will assign it to a less glamorous varnish run.

—Railroad Photographs

. 63 .

NICKEL PLATE POWER

Near Yuton, Illinois, Paul H. Stringham caught this Nickel Plate heavy Mikado, No. 625, wheeling a heavy consist westward. This powerful looking freight power had been recently rebuilt with a stoker, Worthington feed water heater, booster, and pumps on the head end and looms handsomely against a setting sun over the Illinois prairies.

—Railroad Photographs

. 64 .

IN THE VANGUARD OF THE DIESELS

Clattering across the switch points of the Kansas City Terminal, the Chicago, Burlington and Quincy's Pioneer Zephyr sets out on its round trip to Lincoln and Omaha. Made up of a power-baggage unit, a coach, a dinette coach, and a coach-parlor car, the Pioneer Zephyr was placed in service in the fall of 1934 and is still reeling off a daily mileage of 500. It averages forty-three passengers to a run and grosses the Burlington $1.09 a mile. In the field of longevity it ranks every other airflow, light-weight Diesel-powered train in the land.

—Lucius Beebe photograph

. 65 .

IN THE COLORADO UPLANDS

The Exposition Flyer was inaugurated the summer of the San Francisco World's Fair as a through train on fast running time between Chicago and the Pacific Coast over the iron of the Burlington, the Denver and Rio Grande Western, and the Western Pacific. It passed over the Colorado Rockies by way of the Moffat Tunnel by daylight as well as making a daylight run through the spectacular Feather River Canyon of California, and carried coaches, Pullmans, and special diners and observation cars. Here the first section of the Exposition Flyer is shown a few miles west of Denver descending the celebrated approach to the Moffat on the eastbound run. It is powered by one of the Denver and Rio Grande's heavy Mikados or 2-8-2 type specially fitted with a smoke deflector for use on the tunnel run.

—Lucius Beebe photograph

. 66 .

THE NICKEL PLATE LIMITED

In the dense network of railroads that loops south and east from Chicago across northern Indiana, a skein which includes the New York Central, the Pennsylvania, the Baltimore and Ohio, Wabash, Erie and New York, Chicago and St. Louis, the last named swings farther southward than any but the Erie until it crosses the Pennsy at Fort Wayne and curves northward to Buffalo, its eastern terminus. The great bulk of the Nickel Plate's traffic is freight, but this photograph shows the Nickel Plate Limited, eastbound morning varnish out of Chicago, as its driver applies the air for the stop at Englewood, Illinois. At Buffalo its through cars will be hauled to New York over the system of the Lackawanna. Its power is a resplendent Hudson, No. 174, trailing six mail cars, coaches, and Pullmans.

—Lucius Beebe photograph

. 67 .

MAPLELEAF MANIFEST

Because the mapleleaf is the national insignia of the Canadian Dominion, it is also the herald and hallmark of the Canadian National Railways of which the Grand Trunk Line is a subsidiary. This Grand Trunk 2-8-2 No. 3745 is pounding across the Indiana landscape between the Chicago yards and Valparaiso, following the swifter passing of the Mapleleaf, the road's crack varnish on the morning eastbound run.

—Lucius Beebe photograph

. 68 .

MIDLAND AND RED BALL

When the necessity for heavier locomotives with the consequent redistribution of weight made the Mikado outmoded for certain types of freight haul, in 1903 a fifth pair of drivers was added on a series of engines designed for the Atchison, Topeka and Santa Fe to power their heavy drags over the Raton and Glorieta Passes. This 2-10-2 type engine became known as the Santa Fe and is widely used by western railroads to this day. Here is a Chicago and Illinois Midland Santa Fe, photographed by P. H. Stringham, on a southbound fast freight near Pekin, Illinois.

—Railroad Photographs

. 69 .

INTO THE GARDEN

An Alton 2-8-2 or Mikado, blistering from the July run through the Illinois farmlands, rolls down the main ahead of a mixed consist into the East St. Louis yards. The clearboard governing the adjacent iron is set for the Wabash manifest which will shortly start northward on the Chicago fast run.

—Lucius Beebe photograph

. 70 .

NARROW-GAGE PASTORAL

This little 2-8-0 narrow-gage locomotive, carrying white at its markers and with the smoke pouring up through the spark arrester at the top of its stack, is the Rio Grande Southern's No. 42 with No. 41 serving as pusher behind. The train is a westbound extra out of Durango, Colorado, on a two-per-cent grade and it is interesting to notice that on these light little trains the caboose is located before the helper engine instead of behind as is the usual practice with heavier equipment.

—*R. H. Kindig photograph*

. 71 .

ON A BERKSHIRE GRADE

The prototype of the Lima-built 2-8-4 shown here at the head of 120 cars of manifest along the Boston and Albany near Pittsfield, Massachusetts, was the celebrated A-1, a superpower locomotive developed by Lima in 1925 which practically revolutionized freight power on half a dozen railroads. To all appearances, A-1 was just another New York Central Mikado with a second trailing axle under the firebox. But the new 2-8-4 had unsuspected drawbar pull; it developed a sixty per cent increase in cylinder horsepower over the 2-8-2s of comparable axle weight, and it did so with a marked decrease in fuel consumption. Improved features of A-1 were a feed water heater, superheater, limited cut-off making for higher boiler pressure, a booster on the trailer truck, tandem connecting rod assemblies, reducing the work of drive crank pins, and increased air intake space at the ashpan for combustion. The Boston and Albany bought forty-five of the new 2-8-4s, naming them Berkshire-types for the hills through which it hauls its heavy freights, while other roads investing heavily in this power included the Boston and Maine, Illinois Central, Missouri Pacific, Pere Marquette and Detroit, Toledo and Ironton.

—*Railroad Photographs*

. 72 .

VALPARAISO VIGNETTE

Between Chicago Heights and Valparaiso, Indiana, the Pennsylvania's "pan-handle"—over which most of its heavy freights roll in and out of the Chicago classification yards—lies through a mellow countryside providing every known pastoral background for the railroad photographer. This short cut of mixed freight, caboose first, is clattering down the main behind a veteran Consolidation (2-8-0) type locomotive under a July sun. The Pennsy's Class H-10s engines have 62-inch drivers, 205 pounds of steam pressure, and a tractive effort of 61,465 pounds, and are mostly used in local freight and branch-line service.

—Lucius Beebe photograph

. 73 .

"THE THUNDER OF IRREVOCABLE WHEELS"

The Chesapeake and Ohio's No. 3, the Fast Flying Virginian, westbound, rolls at eighty miles an hour into Maysville, Kentucky, once a celebrated river port on the Ohio and now a drowsy midst of mint toddies and wistful souvenirs. Like its companion limiteds, the George Washington and the Sportsman, the F.F.V. is famed for its table fare, the beauty of its standard equipment, and the advertising copy which has made Chessie, the C. & O.'s imaginary kitten, an American household character. The F.F.V. is powered by a heavy-duty Pacific of characteristic C. & O. design with air pumps mounted on the smokebox and headlight centered just above the pilot beam.

—Lucius Beebe photograph

. 74 .

PRESIDENTIAL SPECIAL

Whipping across the Rock Island diamond at Englewood, a few miles south of Chicago, and with white flags flying, this burnished Pennsy K 4s is hauling President M. W. Clement and a posse of ranking railroad officials on an inspection tour to Fort Wayne. The special flyer is made up of the presidential private car, a de luxe Pennsy diner, and an official car fitted with wide windows and favorably elevated seats specially designed for inspection tours of this sort.

—Lucius Beebe photograph

. 75 .

FRESH FROM THE BACK SHOPS

An Atchison, Topeka and Santa Fe heavy Mikado, No. 3189, photographed by V. C. Seaver, Jr., rolling out of Corinth, Illinois, with a mixed consist of heavy freight trailing behind. The Mike had recently been shopped and refitted with a new feed water heater with pump and tank hung on the head end.

—Railroad Photographs

. 76 .

WHEELING THEM THROUGH INDIANA

Hustling along near Valparaiso, Indiana, with a cut of mixed merchandise is this sturdy Pennsylvania 2-10-2 or Santa Fe–type freight hog, Chicago bound. While the Pennsy's steam passenger power is almost entirely limited to its noted K 4s Pacifics and a few Mountain-types, its freight is handled by an assortment of locomotives which includes Consolidations, Mikados, Mountains, Santa Fes, Decapods, and Mallets. This is, of course, because of the power demands of the various geographic terrains encountered in its divisions and the varying density of traffic.

—Lucius Beebe photograph

. 77 .

THE C. & E. I. ZIPPER

At noon each day from the Dearborn Station in Chicago, the Chicago and Eastern Illinois's crack daylight varnish, the St. Louis Zipper, heads southward in competition to the Wabash's Banner Blue, the Alton Limited. On the flat five-hour run through the cornlands of the Middle West, its mail cars, coaches, and Pullmans often top eighty miles an hour, and the beauty of its going is a daily panache to the lives of Nokomis and Sollitt, Goodwine and Hustle and Westervelt. Despite its apparently static pose, the Zipper is here shown making a brisk forty-five at Granite City, Illinois, as it heads for the Merchants' Bridge and the St. Louis terminal. It is powered by a light Pacific, brave with red and gold trim, the main drivers of which is of the new disk design in contrast to the conventional spokes of the other powered wheels.

—Lucius Beebe photograph

. 78 .

A STUDY IN EXHAUSTS

This Missouri Pacific 4-8-2 is pulling the first of two sixteen-car sections of the Sunshine Special up a brief but heavy grade near Webster Groves, Missouri, safety valve popping, smoke exhaust slamming out of the stack and boiler wash blow-off exploding a cloud of live steam against the ballast under the cab.

—Lucius Beebe photograph

. 79 .

A HELPER FOR THE GRADE

Fighting every inch of the way, No. 1341, a Southern Railway System 4-6-2 is at the head end of the westbound Skyland Special as it toils up the 4½ per cent grade east of Saluda, North Carolina. At the rear of the train in this exciting action photograph by W. H. Thrall, Jr., is No. 5028, a 2-10-2 helping push the six mail cars, coaches, and Pullmans of the Special over the hump.

—*Courtesy of Railroad Magazine*

. 80 .

POOL TRAIN'S PROGRESS

Equipped with smoke deflector, all-weather cab, and tank-type tender, this Canadian National Hudson is making time near Vaudreuil, Quebec, ahead of Train No. 5, the La Salle, a pool train between Montreal and Toronto. It was photographed as it scorched the ballast along the manicured C. N. right of way by H. W. Pontin.

—Railroad Photographs

. 81 .

MOUNTAIN DIVISION

In the Cajon Pass, near Victorville, California, this Atchison, Topeka and Santa Fe powerful 2-10-2 freight locomotive with low diameter drive wheels for additional power on the steep grades of the San Bernardino Mountains, is pulling head end on a westbound drag. Farther behind, cut into the middle of the consist and at the rear, are helper engines. The background is typical of the Santa Fe's most spectacular mountain division.

—Courtesy of the Santa Fe

. 82 .

AS BRAKEMEN SEE IT

Passengers accustomed to rubber draft gear and tight locking couplings which eliminate all slack between cars have difficulty in visualizing the violence with which the slack runs on a long string of freight. Without this slack, however, no locomotive yet designed could start a mile of reefers, gondolas, box-cars and tanks; and freight-car couplers are built with approximately a foot of slack to a unit, which means that on a hundred-car train the head of the train is moving at whatever acceleration its locomotive can achieve in a hundred feet before the caboose begins to move. The resulting shock at the rear end of long trains (the Chesapeake and Ohio has run coal drags of 210 cars) has been so great that trainmen have occasionally been injured by being thrown from their positions in the cupolas of old style cabooses with the result that side window cabooses without cupolas are coming into vogue on many lines. This shows the coupling slack between two freight cars at speed on the Wabash Red Ball Freight Train No. 92 as well as the main air line with the handcock at open position.

—Robert Willier photograph

. 83 .

THROUGH THE HAYFIELDS OF ESSEX COUNTY

This unusual looking locomotive with high sand dome, shielded-in smoke-box, and elephant-ear smoke deflectors is no foreign engine, but a somewhat unconventional Pacific, No. 651, hauling the Delaware and Hudson's Laurentian, southbound, at sixty-five miles an hour bound for New York via the New York Central System and Troy. It is characterized by a rotary cam poppet valve gear actuated by standard Walschaerts motion, and its side rigged smoke deflectors are not absolutely unique in American railroading technique since they appear on occasional locomotives of the Pennsylvania and the Boston and Maine. The photograph was taken by Warren G. Fancher in Essex County, New York, famous for its scenic qualities along the west shore of Lake Champlain, and its important rôle in the Indian wars of an earlier era in American history.

—Railroad Photographs

. 84 .

TO CHEYENNE, TO NORTH PLATTE, TO LARAMIE

Compelling names from the legendary past, the main line of the Union Pacific reaches from Omaha to Ogden, and over it flows an immeasurably wealthy portion of the nation's western commerce. Train No. 87, the San Francisco Challenger, westbound, here shown leaving Omaha with the rising sun, is the U. P.'s noted tourist-rate transcontinental haul, furnishing at abated fares what was only yesterday's Pullman luxury equipment. The beautifully maintained and serviced 4-8-4 at the Challenger's head end can haul its sixteen cars of mail and passengers over every grade on the line except Sherman Hill without deviating from an exacting schedule and is typical of the U. P.'s passenger power throughout most of the West.

—Lucius Beebe photograph

. 85 .

DOUBLE-SHOTTED VARNISH

Trailing a mile of heavy smoke exhaust that shrouds its fourteen Pullmans, and double-headed behind a light Pacific helper and a heavy-duty Hudson road engine, the New England States heads westward over the Boston and Albany on the Boston–Chicago run. An all-Pullman, luxury train on the B. & A. and New York Central, this highliner supplants the old Boston section of the Twentieth Century Limited and supplies the most opulent of travel facilities between New England and the Great Lakes. Complete with room cars, lounges, diners, and cafés, it represents, from pilot bar to the gleaming brass of its observation platform, the finest traditions of standard equipment service on a transcontinental haul.

—Lucius Beebe photograph

.86.

The first Mogul or 2-6-0 wheel arrangement type locomotive was built by the Rogers Locomotive and Machine works for the New Jersey Railroad and Transportation Company in 1863. It was the first established variation from the classic American 4-4-0 design, and so great was its reputed power, deriving from the additional pair of drive wheels that it has ever since been known by this romantic name. To-day there are few Moguls in service, but here the photographer's film pack recorded a high-domed Southern Pacific 2-6-0 hauling ten cars noisily up a slight grade, northbound, near Salinas, California. A vanishing type, the Mogul still performs valorously on short freight hauls here and there throughout the land.

—*Lucius Beebe photograph*

. 87 .

THE ALTON LIMITED

No less than four railroads, the Chicago and Eastern Illinois, the Illinois Central, the Wabash, and the Alton (Baltimore and Ohio) are in direct competition on the Chicago–St. Louis run, many of their trains being almost exactly matched for speed and times of departure and arrival at their terminals. Were any of these lines solely or predominantly dependent for their revenue upon this haul, their road to economic suicide would be plainly charted and, even with the greater part of their business deriving from other territories, each of the four carriers suffers in a greater or less degree from the practical quadruplication of its services. Here is the Alton Limited nearing St. Louis in the late afternoon, powered by a competent if not oppressively handsome Pacific, No. 5291.

—*Lucius Beebe photograph*

. 88 .

WESTBOUND: THE WOLVERINE

Of a late summer's afternoon the Boston and Albany's No. 17, the Wolverine, with a leash of twelve coaches and Pullmans, heads into the foothills of the Berkshires in western Massachusetts. It is powered by one of the B. & A.'s heavy-duty Hudsons similar, save for its characteristic square sand dome, in design to the New York Central's equivalent type of motive power. The Wolverine carries Pullman equipment from Boston to Chicago, Detroit, and Grand Rapids and parlor cars and lounges as far as Albany where the B. & A. merges with the parent New York Central System. It is shown here as its hogger notches his throttle at a comfortable seventy near West Brookfield.

—Lucius Beebe photograph

. 89 .

WHERE THREE PER CENT GRADES
ARE COMMONPLACE

These two Denver and Rio Grande Western Mikados (2-8-2 type) with smoke pouring from their stacks as they labor up the spectacular grade leading from Denver to the East Portal of the Moffat Tunnel are hauling twelve cars of the Panoramic, which leaves Denver in the late afternoon and arrives at Salt Lake the next morning at breakfast time. Just as few railroads have more romantic associations and traditions than the D. & R. G. W., so do few have more varied power rosters since its runs include startling grades and mountain divisions of fabulous altitudes. The Panoramic is the companion train, on the Moffat Route, to the Scenic which runs west via the Royal Gorge.

—Vernon Seaver, Jr., photograph

. 90 .

STUDY IN WABASH POWER

The Wabash late afternoon train each way between St. Louis and Chicago complementing the service of the Banner Blue and the night sleeper train, is the Blue Bird. Usually a five- or six-car train, the Blue Bird is here running with ten cars over a summer holiday week-end. It is powered by a light Pacific, No. 662, and an ancient high-wheel, Atlantic-type locomotive, No. 602, and is shown pulling out of Englewood, Illinois, for its fast run to Decatur, where the power will be changed for the haul to St. Louis.

—Lucius Beebe photograph

. 91 .

"AS THE HART PANTETH—"

One of the most potent arguments forwarded by Diesel engineers in favor of the internal combustion motor for train power is the difficulty, in some railroading divisions in the West and Southwest, of obtaining suitable water for steam locomotives. Water in many localities is characterized by such a high mineral content that it must be chemically treated before introducing it to engine boilers and tubes. In some parts of Texas, the Texas and Pacific Railroad pipes its water for distances of 250 miles. In northern states, winter weather creates the problem of preventing water in trackside tanks from freezing, while to avoid the delay of water stops some railroads, like the New York Central, replenish their tenders on fast through trains from track pans, and the Pennsylvania equips its limiteds with tenders whose tanks carry as high as 30,000 gallons at a time. At Lucin, Utah, this Southern Pacific fireman is swinging a water spout over the tank of a Vanderbilt-type tend to fuel the Overland Limited on its westward run toward the High Sierras and the Pacific.

—*Lucius Beebe photograph*

. 92 .

IN DEEPEST INDIANA

Because of the conjunction of its two main lines running between Chicago and Indianapolis and Michigan City and Louisville, at Monon, Indiana, the Chicago, Indianapolis and Louisville Railway is commonly known as the Monon Route. Its three principal daily trains are The Hoosier, Tippecanoe, and Midnight Special. There are also two others in each direction with sleepers between Chicago and Indianapolis and French Lick Springs. On the opposite page is the Hoosier passing through Dyer, Indiana, powered by a light Pacific of characteristic Monon design with its identifying flanged stack.

—Railroad Photographs

. 93 .

THE MOPAC'S NO. 15, THE KAY-SEE FLYER

With his throttle eased well back on its quadrant, the driver of this handsome Missouri Pacific 4-6-2 is wheeling his string of varnish through a cut west of Jefferson City, Missouri. The Pacific-type locomotive was so named because of the first of this wheel arrangement which was built for the Mopac. The Kay-See Flyer makes the St. Louis–Kansas City run in five hours and ten minutes and is a standard-equipment highliner with the conventional coaches, diners, lounge, chair, and observation cars.

—*Lucius Beebe photograph*

. 94 .

SYMBOLS OF INTEGRATED POWER

This is the valve gear and part of the rod assembly of one of the Atchison, Topeka and Santa Fe's 3765 Series, 4-8-4 high-speed passenger locomotives built to the road's specifications by the Baldwin Locomotive Works. The 80-inch drivers are characterized by Baldwin disk-type centers; the piston rods are Standard carbon·steel forgings, and the crank pins on main and intermediate wheels are nickel chromium steel. The valve gear is of the Walschaerts pattern; the main and side rods are chrome nickel molybdenum steel forgings. Three hundred pounds of steam power these locomotives, which are oil-burners, and their tractive force is 66,000 pounds. They are used on the transcontinental hauls of such highliners as The Chief between La Junta and Los Angeles without changing engines.

—Lucius Beebe photograph

. 95 .

ON THE STRAIGHTAWAY

Double heading out of San Bernardino on the run over the Cajon Pass to Barstow, the Santa Fe's Grand Canyon Limited will drop its helper locomotive at
Summit. Here it is shown scorching the ballast on the five-mile straightaway
across the California uplands before hitting the steep grades of the Cajon itself.

—Lucius Beebe photograph

. 96 .

MOPAC PASTORAL

The Missouri Pacific's Train No. 12, the Scenic Limited, eastbound, streaks toward St. Louis through a stand of trees at Kirkwood, Missouri. It is powered by a well-groomed Super-Pacific with shield-type pilot and retractable coupling and carries through cars from Ogden to Atlanta and from Pueblo to New Orleans, as well as a complement of sleepers to be set out at St. Louis. The Mopac plans, as soon as roadbed conditions have been altered to permit higher speed runs, to replace at least two of its steam units on the Kansas City–St. Louis run, where this action shot was taken, with Diesel-powered streamliners, but no lightweight train, whatever its merits of performance, can hold the fascination of the steam power of the spacious railroad tradition.

—*William Barham–Ivan Oaks photograph*

. 97 .

"THERE ISN'T A TRAIN I WOULDN'T TAKE
NO MATTER WHERE IT'S GOING"

No railroad in the United States has about it more romantic associations than the Denver and Rio Grande Western which had its origins in the spacious silver times of Colorado's youth. To-day it flourishes as the principal trunk line crossing the Rocky Mountains between Denver and Salt Lake City where it meets the Western Pacific. This is the D. & R. G. W.'s Train No. 1, the Scenic Limited, a de luxe varnish on the Royal Gorge run, hitting fifty near Sedalia, Colorado. The power is a 4-8-4 or Northern locomotive with a leash of mail cars and coaches, Pullmans, lounge, and observation cars. The line's two other daily passenger trains to Salt Lake, the Panoramic and the Exposition Flyer, now a permanent institution, are routed via the Moffat Tunnel.

—Lucius Beebe photograph

THE CENTURY, BOSTON SECTION

Until it was supplanted by the New England States, the Boston section of the Twentieth Century Limited ran over the iron of the Boston and Albany to Albany where it joined the main section rolling west from New York. With the inaugural of the streamlined Century, however, the Boston section was discontinued because of dissimilarity of equipment and because there was insufficient New England traffic for an extra-fare, all-Pullman run, and its traffic was taken over by the New England States, an all-Pullman, regular-fare flyer on the straight Boston–Chicago haul. This shows the old Boston section of the Century burning up the ballast behind a mighty B. & A. Hudson near Pittsfield, Massachusetts, in the midst of the Berkshire Hills.

—Lucius Beebe photograph

. 99 .

GOLDEN GATE

Near Fresno, California, the Santa Fe's Golden Gate, one of two streamlined Diesel-powered flyers on the Bakersfield–San Fransico run, coördinating at Bakersfield with bus service to Los Angeles, hits sixty against a background of California fruit trees. The two Golden Gates cover a total of 626 miles daily and have been in service since July, 1938. Each unit includes seven cars under ordinary operating conditions, although only six are shown in this action shot. They are a power unit, a baggage-chair car, a chair-club-bar car, a lunch-counter-restaurant car, a coach, and a chair-observation-lounge. This Santa Fe run through the middle of inland California was instituted in direct competition with the run of the Espee's Daylight on the Coast Division.

—Courtesy of the Santa Fe

. 100 .

NEARING THE END OF THE RUN

Over the route of the New York Central and the Big Four, the Central's South-western Limited rolls daily from New York to St. Louis in opposition to the Pennsylvania's fleet passenger hauls over a somewhat shorter right of way. Here it is shown headed by one of the Central's famed Hudsons of a series only slightly older than that which powers the Twentieth Century Limited approaching St. Louis with eleven cars behind, the last two, a sleeper and observation lounge, of the airflow design originally built for service on the Century.

—Lucius Beebe photograph

. 101 .

THUNDER AT DAWN

Trailing an impressive exhaust of steam and white smoke against a winter sky, this Pacific of the Southern Railway is hauling Train No. 5, the Florida Sunbeam, over a bridge on the Cincinnati, New Orleans and Texas Pacific, a mile south of Ludlow, Kentucky. The photograph, taken by Thomas O. Acree, is on what is known as the Erlanger Grade where the line ascends into the Kentucky Mountains and where heavy mail and passenger trains are often double-headed. On engine No. 6482 there is visible the smoke deflector characteristic of the motive power used on this division, where tunnels are extremely numerous.

—Thomas O. Acree photograph

A STUDY IN SILVER AND SCARLET

The Chicago, Rock Island and Pacific's Peoria Rocket smashes its trucks across the Pennsy diamond at Englewood, Illinois, on the first of its two daily round trips on the Chicago–Peoria runs which add up to a total mileage of 644 at an overall scheduled speed of 60.1 miles an hour. Painted an eye-filling crimson and silver, the Peoria unit of the Rock Island's fleet of Rockets is made up of five cars, a power car, a baggage-dinette, two coaches, and an observation-lounge. Its revenue per train mile is $1.65 which makes it the most profitable of the six Rockets maintained by the road.

—Lucius Beebe photograph

. 103 .

THE SYMBOLS AND THE SUBSTANCE

The Burlington's passenger lines from Hannibal and the Northwest enter St. Louis on the west side of the Mississippi, but its freight rolls into East St. Louis along with that of the Alton and Wabash from the North and Chicago. Here is a Burlington 2-8-2, freshly shopped and with its smokebox newly silvered, rolling ahead of a mixed consist under the east approach to the Merchant's Bridge into the ordered confusion of the East St. Louis classification yards. On either side of the photograph are the symbols of the two indispensable factors in modern railroading, the automatic block signal system's semaphore and the slender fabric of the illimitable telegraph lines.

—Lucius Beebe photograph

(2)